This Journal Belongs to

....

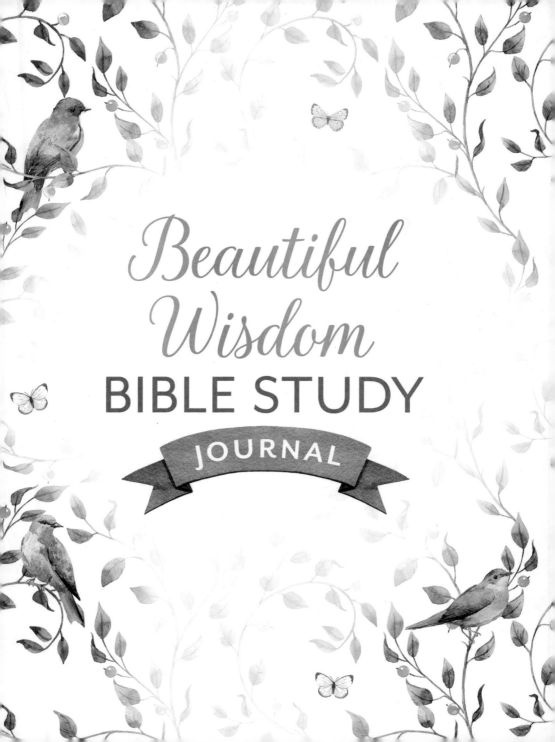

Beautiful Wisdom
BIBLE STUDY
JOURNAL

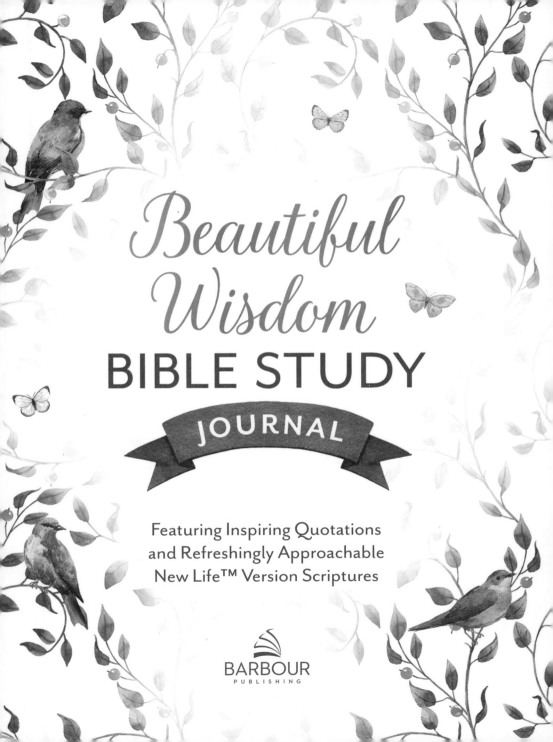

Beautiful Wisdom

BIBLE STUDY

JOURNAL

Featuring Inspiring Quotations
and Refreshingly Approachable
New Life™ Version Scriptures

BARBOUR
PUBLISHING

ISBN 978-1-63609-273-7

Published by Barbour Publishing, Inc., 1810 Barbour Drive, Uhrichsville, Ohio 44683, www.barbourbooks.com

Our mission is to inspire the world with the life-changing message of the Bible.

Printed in China.

You want the most from your time in God's Word. . .

The *Beautiful Wisdom Bible Study Journal* provides encouraging and edifying quotations, refreshingly approachable New Life Version scriptures, and ample space for you to jot down your reflections.

This journal will provoke thought and allow you to share your own insights, creating a treasured record of your personal walk with God.

God showed His love to us. While we were still sinners, Christ died for us.

ROMANS 5:8

God's love, pouring through the lonely life of Jesus, runs deeper, wider, and farther than any loneliness of the human heart.
BONNIE KEEN

"Get your life from Me and I will live in you. No branch can give fruit by itself. It has to get life from the vine. You are able to give fruit only when you have life from Me."

JOHN 15:4

To abide with Christ—to stay with Him and to learn from Him—is to continually receive eyes to see, ears to hear, and a heart to obey.
ANGELA THOMAS MCGUFFEY

The Holy Spirit works in each person in one way or another for the good of all.
1 CORINTHIANS 12:7

You abound in talents, abilities, and skills. Which gifts of yours enrich you and the lives of those around you?
VIRGINIA ANN FROEHLE

So if we stay here on earth or go home to Him, we always want to please Him.

2 CORINTHIANS 5:9

God's opinion is the only one that matters, and His pleasure isn't necessarily measured in book sales, income generated, or pats on the back from others.
ROBIN CHADDOCK

I am allowed to do all things, but not everything is good for me to do! Even if I am free to do all things, I will not do them if I think it would be hard for me to stop when I know I should.

1 CORINTHIANS 6:12

God created us with a need to be fed
and filled, yet our desires seemingly go unmet....
Left unchecked, our misplaced contentment crashes
into our empty lives as we attempt to fill up on "treasures"
that devastate not only our pocketbooks but also our souls.
MARSHA CROCKETT

My soul will be proud to tell about the Lord. Let those who suffer hear it and be filled with joy. Give great honor to the Lord with me. Let us praise His name together.

PSALM 34:2–3

Whatever tragedy has befallen you—first, allow God to comfort your heart, and then permit Him to use it as a way to point others to Christ.
REBECCA LUSIGNOLO

"We beg you to ask God if all will go well..."

JUDGES 18:5

Whose advice are you taking and whose example are you watching?
ANNE GRAHAM LOTZ

We do not want anyone to give up because of troubles. You know that we can expect troubles.

1 THESSALONIANS 3:3

Affliction is the opener of the understanding.
ELISABETH ELLIOT

....
....
....
....
....
....
....
....
....
....
....
....
....
....
....
....
....
....
....
....
....
....
....
....
....
....
....
....
....

"Even when you are old I will be the same. And even when your hair turns white, I will help you. I will take care of what I have made. I will carry you, and will save you."

ISAIAH 46:4

*Look, my feet hurt some mornings, and my
body is less forgiving when I exercise more
than I am used to. But I love my life more....
It's not that I think less of myself, but that I think
of myself less often. And that feels like heaven to me.*
ANNE LAMOTT

"Instead, go after the holy nation of God. Then all these other things will be given to you."

LUKE 12:31

What's my goal? What's my ambition?
Is it my happiness or my holiness?
KAY ARTHUR

*If you are angry, do not let it become sin. Get
over your anger before the day is finished.*

EPHESIANS 4:26

Speaking in anger is classified as careless because when we speak in anger, we are not thinking of the consequences of our words.
RHONDA RIZZO WEBB

"Honest words give pain. But what does your arguing prove?"

JOB 6:25

Getting into arguments is part of being human; it's not wrong. Enjoying the arguments, actively seeking them out for the pleasure of arguing, is wrong.
SUZETTE HADEN ELGIN

Be strong. Be strong in heart, all you who hope in the Lord.

PSALM 31:24

There is no safer place for your hopes and dreams than in the loving hands of your faithful Father.
LESLIE LUDY

*Keep your heart pure for out of it are
the important things of life.*

PROVERBS 4:23

Find the gold. Whatever has happened to you in the past, and whatever is happening in your life now, look for the hidden blessing, the lesson to be learned, or the character trait to be forged. Trust that, since God has allowed these experiences, somewhere there is gold for you.
ELIZABETH GEORGE

When you were baptized, you were buried as Christ was buried. When you were raised up in baptism, you were raised as Christ was raised. You were raised to a new life by putting your trust in God. It was God Who raised Jesus from the dead.

COLOSSIANS 2:12

Most of what we do in worldly life is geared toward our staying dry, looking good, not going under. But in baptism. . .you agree to do something that's a little sloppy. . . . It's about surrender.
ANNE LAMOTT

He has made everything beautiful in its time.

ECCLESIASTES 3:11

Beauty brings us into places of healing,
as well as into God's presence.
JANE RUBIETTA

....
....
....
....
....
....
....
....
....
....
....
....
....
....
....
....
....
....
....
....
....
....
....

You know, and so does God, how pure and right and without blame we were among you who believe.

1 THESSALONIANS 2:10

Our conduct has a direct influence on how people think about the Gospel. The world doesn't judge us by our theology; the world judges us by our behavior.
CAROLYN MAHANEY

"For sure, I tell you, he who puts his trust in Me has life that lasts forever."

JOHN 6:47

Foundations to be reliable must always be unshakable.
HANNAH WHITALL SMITH

"For sure, I tell you, whoever gives you a cup of water to drink in My name because you belong to Christ will not lose his reward from God."

MARK 9:41

The New Covenant is our guarantee of belonging,
of never being forsaken, of never being alone.
KAY ARTHUR

Your Word have I hid in my heart,
that I may not sin against You.
PSALM 119:11

Memorization is a very valuable tool in the Christian life, and God will use it in a mighty way if we choose to memorize His Word.
CAROLE LEWIS

*Let us honor and thank the God and Father
of our Lord Jesus Christ. He has already
given us a taste of what heaven is like.*

EPHESIANS 1:3

God doesn't bless us so that we'll know He's faithful—we trust in His faithfulness and then discover His blessings.
KARON PHILLIPS

The gifts on an altar that God wants are a broken spirit. O God, You will not hate a broken heart and a heart with no pride.

PSALM 51:17

God wants you to know that when everything else is gone, that makes more room for Him, and every time there is more room for Him, you are blessed.
ANGELA THOMAS

If one part of the body suffers, all the other parts suffer with it. If one part is given special care, the other parts are happy.

1 CORINTHIANS 12:26

Our friends hurt because we hurt. And their love flows into us. That is burden-bearing.
LUCI SHAW

O Lord, stand by me for I have lived my life without blame. I have trusted in the Lord without changing.

PSALM 26:1

Character is not given to us; we build it ourselves.
MABEL HALE

"For sure, I tell you, whoever does not receive the holy nation of God as a little child does not go into it."

MARK 10:15

I may have destroyed my own future, but God is always the perfect past, present and future. He still desires to restore childlikeness to my battered, aged soul. "Let's play," He calls. "Where are you?"
KAREN BURTON MAINS

See, children are a gift from the Lord.
The children born to us are our special reward.
PSALM 127:3

Caring for children is an extremely valuable skill that is scarce these days. It may be the most significant gift you could choose to spend your life giving.
VALERIE BELL

"Choose today whom you will serve. . . . But as for me and my family, we will serve the Lord."

JOSHUA 24:15

The Lord is forever faithful to His decision to give us free will. It's always our choice what we allow into our lives.
KARON PHILLIPS

"Come to Me, all of you who work and have heavy loads. I will give you rest."

MATTHEW 11:28

When we approach Christ, open our clenching fists, and lay down our armor of work and fatigue, we find again that oneness with Him, that irreplaceable rhythm of trust and toil.
JANE RUBIETTA

Be holy in every part of your life. Be like the Holy One Who chose you.

1 PETER 1:15

To have peace with God one must intentionally die to self, to all self ambition, until you are only living for Jesus.
KATHRYN KUHLMAN

"The Lord gave and the Lord has taken away. Praise the name of the Lord."

JOB 1:21

*Our lives are shaped less by what
actually happens to us than by the
meaning we ascribe to these events.*
MICHELE WEINER-DAVIS

He gives us comfort in all our troubles. Then we can comfort other people who have the same troubles. We give the same kind of comfort God gives us.

2 CORINTHIANS 1:4

We must set our faces like a flint to believe, under each and every sorrow and trial, in the divine Comforter, and to accept and rejoice in His all-embracing comfort.
HANNAH WHITALL SMITH

All those who put their trust in Christ were together and shared what they owned.

ACTS 2:44

People are yearning to discover community.
We have had enough loneliness,
independence and competition.
THEA JARVIS

When He got out of the boat, He saw many people. He
had loving-pity for them and healed those who were sick.

MATTHEW 14:14

One of the most powerful ways to gain entrance into someone's heart is to serve them.
MELODY ROSSI

"Now who is willing to give himself and be set apart today to the Lord?"

1 CHRONICLES 29:5

Satan sometimes suggests that an offering will satisfy God, when in fact He is demanding our all.
CORRIE TEN BOOM

A God-like life gives us much when we are happy for what we have.

1 TIMOTHY 6:6

By trying to grab fulfillment everywhere, we find it nowhere.
ELISABETH ELLIOT

"Have I not told you? Be strong and have strength of heart! Do not be afraid or lose faith. For the Lord your God is with you anywhere you go."

JOSHUA 1:9

Having courage for the long haul means embracing God's love in the face of unrelenting difficulty.
CAROL KENT

"Write in a book all the words which I have spoken to you."

JEREMIAH 30:2

I never sat down to write without first praying that I might not be suffered to write anything that would do harm, and that, on the contrary, I might be taught to say what would do good.
ELIZABETH PRENTISS

He carried our sins in His own body when He died on a cross. In doing this, we may be dead to sin and alive to all that is right and good. His wounds have healed you!

1 PETER 2:24

Take a long look at what happened at Calvary.
The agony there was of the just for the unjust.
ELISABETH ELLIOT

We are sure we will be glad to be free of these bodies. It will be good to be at home with the Lord.

2 CORINTHIANS 5:8

*I do not wait for the under-
taker, but for the Uptaker.*
CORRIE TEN BOOM

*Keep Your promise to Your servant, the promise
You made to those who fear and worship You.*

PSALM 119:38

God loves you unconditionally, Beloved. The question is: Do you love Him unconditionally?
KAY ARTHUR

The little troubles we suffer now for a short time are making us ready for the great things God is going to give us forever.

2 CORINTHIANS 4:17

*We have a promise and a hope to hold
when times are hard and understanding is
dim—one day we will be home, where tears
and fears are no more, joy and delight are forever
ours, leaning into the loving arms of our heavenly Father.*
TAMARA BOGGS

I cried with all my heart. Answer me,
O Lord! I will keep Your Law.
PSALM 119:145

The fact is—and both scripture and experience make this clear—that no man or woman can completely fill another person's emotional tank. That's a God-sized task meant for. . .well, God.
CINDI MCMENAMIN

"This is life that lasts forever. It is to know You, the only true God, and to know Jesus Christ Whom You have sent."

JOHN 17:3

You know, eternal life does not start when you go to heaven. It starts the moment you reach out to Jesus. That is where it all begins!
CORRIE TEN BOOM

For a man who is right with God falls seven times,
and rises again, but the sinful fall in time of trouble.
PROVERBS 24:16

*Our perception of success and failure may,
in fact be inaccurate. . .perhaps the almighty
God has chosen to work through us without
letting us know. We may find out years later that
what we saw as failure was actually God's success.*
ALICE FRYLING

Our life is lived by faith. We do not live by what we see in front of us.
2 CORINTHIANS 5:7

Great faith believes in God even when
He plays His hand close to his vest, never
showing all His cards.... God wants to increase
your "measure of faith." He does this whenever
He conceals a matter, and you trust Him nevertheless.
JONI EARECKSON TADA

"We must obey God instead of men!"
ACTS 5:29

Never agree to do something in order to impress people or because you fear what they may think or say about you if you don't.
JOYCE MEYER

"O Lord our God, You are kind and forgiving, even when we would not obey You."

DANIEL 9:9

The hardest person to forgive is yourself. If it seems impossible to do, remember that God forgives everyone, over and over, so for you to refuse yourself forgiveness is to set yourself above God.
BARBARA BARTOCCI

"If you forgive people their sins, your Father in heaven will forgive your sins also."

MATTHEW 6:14

*Forgiveness has little to do with what was done
to us, but much to do with what we choose to do
with it. I believe it is the ultimate expression of love.*
SHARON JAYNES

"You will know the truth and the truth will make you free."

JOHN 8:32

When God gave us the gift of freedom, He placed it within a framework. He also gave us a well-defined guideline for the effective use of this gift.
GIGI GRAHAM TCHIVIDJIAN

A friend loves at all times.
PROVERBS 17:17

A person is made better or worse by his friends.
MABEL HALE

But the fruit that comes from having the Holy Spirit in our lives is: love, joy, peace, not giving up, being kind, being good, having faith, being gentle, and being the boss over our own desires. The Law is not against these things.

GALATIANS 5:22–23

*You can't be a born again child of God and
produce fruit from hell all of your life.*
LISA MENDENHALL

There are different kinds of gifts. But it is the same Holy Spirit Who gives them.

1 CORINTHIANS 12:4

Blessedness is a gift of God, which cannot be taken away by the chances and changes of this life, because it has been given by God.
SUSAN JOHNSON

When Abram was ninety-nine years old, the Lord came to him and said, "I am God All-powerful. Obey Me, and be without blame."

GENESIS 17:1

For all those dark times, here's a word of hope: God meets us where we are. Even if we aren't looking in His direction, He is always looking in ours.
LIZ CURTIS HIGGS

"For as the heavens are higher than the earth, so are My ways higher than your ways, and My thoughts than your thoughts."

ISAIAH 55:9

*Seeing God as merely an elevated form
of ourselves sets us up for failure.*
PAM FARREL

*May the loving-favor of the Lord Jesus
Christ be with your spirit.*
PHILEMON 25

When a believer has been steeped in grace,
all the members of his or her immediate
society detect a refreshing fragrance.
CHRISTINE WOOD

Show me loving-kindness, O Lord, for I am in trouble. My eyes, my soul and my body are becoming weak from being sad.

PSALM 31:9

We move toward healing when we choose to inch our foot out the door of our own grief and back into the day-to-day happenings of life.
JOAN GUNTZELMAN

Grow in the loving-favor that Christ gives you.
Learn to know our Lord Jesus Christ better.

2 PETER 3:18

Only you will ever limit what you are for God.
KAY ARTHUR

If you do not have wisdom, ask God for it. He is always ready to give it to you and will never say you are wrong for asking.

JAMES 1:5

If I have done anything in my life, it has been easy because the Master has gone before.
MARY SLESSOR

Yes, happy are the people whose God is the Lord!

PSALM 144:15

When the dream planted in our heart is one that God has planted there, a strange happiness flows into us. At that moment all of the spiritual resources of the universe are released to help us.
CATHERINE MARSHALL

Take your share of suffering as a
good soldier of Jesus Christ.
2 TIMOTHY 2:3

God is more concerned with our condition than our comfort, and He will allow things to become uncomfortable in our lives to expose our true condition. He would rather have us temporarily uncomfortable than eternally tormented.
LISA BEVERE

Jesus went on to all the towns and cities. He taught in their places of worship. He preached the Good News of the holy nation of God. He healed every sickness and disease the people had.

MATTHEW 9:35

No, I do not know why all are not healed physically, but all can be healed spiritually, and that's the greatest miracle any human being can know.
KATHRYN KUHLMAN

I heard a loud voice coming from heaven. It said, "See! God's home is with men. He will live with them. They will be His people. God Himself will be with them. He will be their God."

REVELATION 21:3

Make no mistake about it! Heaven is a home populated by the Lord and His loved ones who have made the deliberate choice to be there.
ANNE GRAHAM LOTZ

May you have loving-favor from our Lord
Jesus Christ. May you have the love of God.
May you be joined together by the Holy Spirit.
2 CORINTHIANS 13:14

Allow yourself to be led by the Spirit of God. That Spirit will unerringly conduct you to the end purpose for which your soul was created. . .the enjoyment of God.
JEANNE GUYON

*Be happy to have people stay for
the night and eat with you.*

1 PETER 4:9

Ideally, hospitality is the outward expression of an inner attitude, a virtue that erupts from the heart, spilling out toward others.
THEA JARVIS

*The fear of the Lord is the teaching for wisdom,
and having no pride comes before honor.*

PROVERBS 15:33

One can so easily become too great to be used by God. One can never be too small for His service.
CORRIE TEN BOOM

"Those who are hungry and thirsty to be right with God are happy, because they will be filled."

MATTHEW 5:6

*Collectively and individually, we are crying
for the solace of reconnection with God.*
SUE PATTON THOELE

"Do not be as those who pretend to be someone they are not."

MATTHEW 6:5

Before you act, know your motivation.
MARTHA BOLTON

And God made man in His own likeness. In the likeness of God He made him. He made both male and female.

GENESIS 1:27

Human beings need reminders that we are not "just mortals." We are created in the image of God with value and dignity.
LYNN ANDERSON

The honor of good people will lead them.

PROVERBS 11:3

The world is looking for people who really believe and live what they say.
KAY ARTHUR

*See what great love the Father has for us
that He would call us His children.*
1 JOHN 3:1

To have a nodding acquaintance with the Creator of the universe is no small thought. But to be on intimate terms with Him is enough to give us heart flutters for the rest of our lives.
JOY DAWSON

Jesus said to His followers, "If anyone wants to be My follower, he must forget about himself. He must take up his cross and follow Me."

MATTHEW 16:24

Following God is always the best choice.
It is the safest choice, although it feels
anything but safe in the chaos of change.
MARY ANN FROEHLICH

As He saw many people, He had loving-pity on them. They were troubled and were walking around everywhere. They were like sheep without a shepherd.

MATTHEW 9:36

*The Gospel accounts show [Jesus] with a
passion for helping those in trouble. He has
not changed. The minute we need saving from
anything, He stands ready in His role as Savior.*
CATHERINE MARSHALL

*Be glad in the Lord and be full of joy, you who are right
with God! Sing for joy all you who are pure in heart!*

PSALM 32:11

Joy is not the fruit of "favorable" circumstances.
Rather, it's the outpouring of a contented heart.
WENDY WIDDER

*Do the right thing for the weak and those
without a father. Stand up for the rights
of those who are suffering and in need.*

PSALM 82:3

No cruelty, no crime, no injustice escapes the attention of God.
KAY ARTHUR

You should be kind to others and have no pride.
Be gentle and be willing to wait for others.
COLOSSIANS 3:12

Pour honey into hearts instead of vinegar.
AMY NAPPA

Then your lives will please the Lord. You will do every kind of good work, and you will know more about God.

COLOSSIANS 1:10

Learning who God is is not a lecture but a lab.
KARON PHILLIPS

....

....

....

....

....

....

....

....

....

....

....

....

....

....

....

....

....

....

....

....

....

....

....

A glad heart is good medicine, but a broken spirit dries up the bones.

PROVERBS 17:22

Laughing at ourselves is a sign that our
spirit transcends the present trouble.
We believe that this life is not all there is.
We believe that our God will look after us.
ANNE BRYAN SMOLLIN

We know that God makes all things work together for the good of those who love Him and are chosen to be a part of His plan.

ROMANS 8:28

Life is not a series of accidents but a succession of divine appointments.
MARY SOUTHERLAND

You do not know about tomorrow. What is your life? It is like fog. You see it and soon it is gone.

JAMES 4:14

The second half of life is a chance to get our priorities straight. It's a time to realize that having the last word isn't as important as having a conversation.
MARTHA BOLTON

God is love.
1 JOHN 4:8

Nothing in me can surprise [God] out of loving me. . .there is wonderful comfort in that.
AMY CARMICHAEL

Marriage should be respected by everyone.
HEBREWS 13:4

Marriage becomes what we create and put in instead of what we expect and take out.
SUSANNA MCMAHON

We pray that you will become strong Christians.
2 CORINTHIANS 13:9

Maturity in Christ is. . .not about finally attaining some level of pseudo-perfection. It is about remaining in the arms of God. Abiding and staying, even in my weakness, even in my failure.
ANGELA THOMAS

I will think about Your Law and have respect for Your ways.

PSALM 119:15

When God dwells at the center of our lives, peace and contentment will belong to us just as surely as we belong to God.
BETH MOORE

The Lord is full of loving-kindness and pity.
JAMES 5:11

Guilt is darkness; mercy is light.
LISA BEVERE

The love of money is the beginning of all kinds of sin.
Some people have turned from the faith because of their
love for money. They have made much pain
for themselves because of this.

1 TIMOTHY 6:10

Prosperity is really a matter of attitude, not an amount of money. Money doesn't cause problems. People who fall in love with it do.
VICKI KUYPER

"Can a woman forget her nursing child? Can she have no pity on the son to whom she gave birth?"

ISAIAH 49:15

Being a mother truly is an assignment from God which He uses, for instance, to make us more Christlike by giving us countless opportunities to die to our self.
ELIZABETH GEORGE

"It is better to obey than to give gifts. It is better to listen than to give the fat of rams."

1 SAMUEL 15:22

Obedience, when it flows out of a genuine love for
Jesus Christ, is never wasted and never regretted.
LESLIE LUDY

Do not be too hard on your children so they will become angry. Teach them in their growing years with Christian teaching.

EPHESIANS 6:4

If you pretend to be perfect and demand that your children join in the pretense, they will not be able to turn to you when they fail.
CONNIE NEAL

Work for the Lord with a heart full of love for Him.

ROMANS 12:11

It is not the place where we are, or the work that we do or cannot do, that matters, it is something else. It is the fire within that burns and shines, whatever be our circumstances.
AMY CARMICHAEL

He has taken our sins from us as far as the east is from the west.

PSALM 103:12

God only looks at your future because
He's canceled out your past.
KARON PHILLIPS

You must be willing to wait without giving up.
HEBREWS 10:36

Nothing so cultivates the grace of patience as the endurance of temptation.
HANNAH WHITALL SMITH

After you have suffered for awhile, God Himself will make you perfect. He will keep you in the right way. He will give you strength. He is the God of all loving-favor and has called you through Christ Jesus to share His shining-greatness forever.

1 PETER 5:10

God knows we won't be perfect today. Complete perfection is reserved for a time in the future. We're not done yet. If we were done, we'd be dead.
ELISA MORGAN

Let us keep looking to Jesus. Our faith comes from Him and He is the One Who makes it perfect. He did not give up when He had to suffer shame and die on a cross. He knew of the joy that would be His later. Now He is sitting at the right side of God.

HEBREWS 12:2

If things upset, irritate, or even momentarily bother me, let me think of what Christ endured for me and the contrast will put my troubles in perspective.
ELISABETH ELLIOT

Is anyone among you suffering? He should pray.
Is anyone happy? He should sing songs of thanks to God.

JAMES 5:13

Fretting magnifies the problem,
but prayer magnifies God.
JOANNA WEAVER

Let us go with complete trust to the throne of God. We will receive His loving-kindness and have His loving-favor to help us whenever we need it.

HEBREWS 4:16

The desire to be with God, to know Him, and to draw from Him is among our most primal. Yet, we do more than desire Him. We need him. Just as we cannot live without water, we cannot live without God's presence.
EVA MARIE EVERSON

*Pride comes before being destroyed and
a proud spirit comes before a fall.*

PROVERBS 16:18

Entitlement is born in each of our hearts the moment soul satisfaction in God is swallowed by self-satisfaction.
SHELLY BEACH

Jesus said to her, "Martha, Martha, you are worried and troubled about many things. Only a few things are important, even just one. Mary has chosen the good thing. It will not be taken away from her."

LUKE 10:41–42

At the end of our life will we really care about
all the hours we worked, all the committees we
sat on, or even all the money we accumulated? Or
will we wish we had spent more time laughing, talking
to loved ones, relaxing, and filling our hearts and souls with
life-giving memories? My guess is that we would choose the latter.
ANNE BRYAN SMOLLIN

"The Lord your God has chosen you out of all the nations on the earth, to be His own."

DEUTERONOMY 7:6

Reject low living, sight walking, small planning, casual praying, and limited giving—God has chosen you for greatness.
ANNE GRAHAM LOTZ

You have been given a new birth. It was from a seed that cannot die. This new life is from the Word of God which lives forever.

1 PETER 1:23

The Lord never wastes anything. He will take everything old and create for you something new.
KARON PHILLIPS

Religion that is pure and good before God the Father is to help children who have no parents and to care for women whose husbands have died who have troubles. Pure religion is also to keep yourself clean from the sinful things of the world.

JAMES 1:27

You have to overcome your religiosity that substitutes positive thinking for holiness, rituals for repentance, traditions for truth, and orthodoxy for obedience.
ANNE GRAHAM LOTZ

Let us do our best to go into that rest.
HEBREWS 4:11

Rest is an internal state of soul, a relaxing into God's chest even when dashing through a day or a season.
JANE RUBIETTA

....
....
....
....
....
....
....
....
....
....
....
....
....
....
....
....
....
....
....
....
....
....
....

I ask you from my heart to give your bodies to God because of His loving-kindness to us. Let your bodies be a living and holy gift given to God. He is pleased with this kind of gift. This is the true worship that you should give Him.

ROMANS 12:1

I will offer to Him both my tears and my exultation. Nothing we offer to Him will be lost.
ELISABETH ELLIOT

God planned to save us from the punishment of sin through our Lord Jesus Christ. He did not plan for us to suffer from His anger.

1 THESSALONIANS 5:9

God's salvation is not a purchase to
be made, nor wages to be earned, nor
a summit to be climbed, nor a task to be
accomplished; but it is simply and only a gift to
be accepted, and can only be accepted by faith.
HANNAH WHITALL SMITH

You were chosen by God the Father long ago. He knew you were to become His children. You were set apart for holy living by the Holy Spirit. May you obey Jesus Christ and be made clean by His blood. May you be full of His loving-favor and peace.

1 PETER 1:2

Sanctification is not a heavy yoke,
but a joyful liberation.
CORRIE TEN BOOM

O God, You are my God. I will look for You with all my heart and strength. My soul is thirsty for You. My flesh is weak wanting You in a dry and tired land where there is no water.

PSALM 63:1

All over the world, people go to unimaginable lengths to find God—which is sad when you consider the unimaginable lengths God has already gone to find us.
JOANNA WEAVER

I will give thanks to You, for the greatness of the way I was made brings fear. Your works are great and my soul knows it very well.

PSALM 139:14

A healthy self-image is not one of pride or arrogance, but one that coincides with God's viewpoint. . . . In His eyes, every person is valuable.
MARY SOUTHERLAND

Do your best to add holy living to your faith. Then add to this a better understanding. As you have a better understanding, be able to say no when you need to. Do not give up. And as you wait and do not give up, live God-like.

2 PETER 1:5–6

We want to change our out-of-control behavior.
The danger in wanting to change, however, is
being impatient and naïve about the process.
KAREN O'CONNOR

There is a time to tear apart, and a time to sew together; a time to be quiet, and a time to speak.

ECCLESIASTES 3:7

*Quiet is a blessed gift. In this frantic world
how we must cherish every moment of it, and
carve it out for ourselves every chance we get.*
ANNE ORTLUND

*You get what is coming to you when you sin.
It is death! But God's free gift is life that lasts
forever. It is given to us by our Lord Jesus Christ.*

ROMANS 6:23

Wherever sin is present, war is raging.
JAN WINEBRENNER AND DEBRA FRAZIER

In the morning before the sun was up, Jesus went to a place where He could be alone. He prayed there.

MARK 1:35

The longing for solitude is the longing for God.
RUTH HALEY BARTON

But I am suffering and in pain. O God, may
You save me and set me up on high.
PSALM 69:29

When you are hurting, your head says that God is far away, but Jesus says, in fact, that God is closer than ever.
ANGELA THOMAS

May the God of peace set you apart for Himself. May every part of you be set apart for God. May your spirit and your soul and your body be kept complete. May you be without blame when our Lord Jesus Christ comes again.

1 THESSALONIANS 5:23

How are we transformed? By the renewing of our mind. By convincing our heart that God is good, even when our circumstances are not.
DONNA PARTOW

Do not be fooled. You cannot fool God.
A man will get back whatever he plants!
GALATIANS 6:7

For good or for bad we will harvest what we plant, more than we plant, later than we plant.
REBECCA LUSIGNOLO

Speak with them in such a way they will want to listen to you. Do not let your talk sound foolish. Know how to give the right answer to anyone.

COLOSSIANS 4:6

If you can't say something nice,
take a vow of silence.
MARTHA BOLTON

Give all your worries to Him because He cares for you.

1 PETER 5:7

By itself, stress won't destroy our families;
but the way we handle it can.
SANDRA ALDRICH

You were living without Christ then.... You had nothing
in this world to hope for. You were without God.

EPHESIANS 2:12

We are designed to function poorly, to feel over-whelmed and alone apart from our relationship with Jesus. We are made to be lost without God.
ANGELA THOMAS MCGUFFEY

....

....

....

....

....

....

....

....

....

....

....

....

....

....

....

....

....

....

....

....

....

....

O Lord, we beg You to save us! O Lord, we ask that You let everything go well for us!

PSALM 118:25

True achievement only exists when our confidence comes from God and our gain results from a life of integrity.
PAM FARREL

Your Word has given me new life.
This is my comfort in my suffering.
PSALM 119:50

The deepest lessons come out of the deepest waters and the hottest fires.
ELISABETH ELLIOT

Remember that our fathers on earth punished us. We had respect for them. How much more should we obey our Father in heaven and live?

HEBREWS 12:9

The discipline of surrender. . .has nothing to do with bondage. It is an expression of freedom.
KAREN O'CONNOR

"Go and make followers of all the nations. Baptize them in the name of the Father and of the Son and of the Holy Spirit."

MATTHEW 28:19

If we want to be disciple makers, then, we must follow Jesus' example and intentionally seek out those who are waiting to grow.
ALICE FRYLING

You should be happy when you have all kinds of tests. You know these prove your faith. It helps you not to give up.

JAMES 1:2–3

Just as God allowed Job, John the Baptist, and many other faithful believers to be tested and troubled beyond their human strength, He may test us.
LESLIE HASKIN

I will give a gift of thanks to You and call on the name of the Lord.

PSALM 116:17

We can thank God for everything good,
and all the rest we don't comprehend yet.
KRISTIN ARMSTRONG

*We break down every thought and proud thing
that puts itself up against the wisdom of God. We
take hold of every thought and make it obey Christ.*

2 CORINTHIANS 10:5

Often, we allow our thoughts to shape us, rather than consciously choosing to shape our thoughts.
SHELLY BEACH

The tongue is also a small part of the body, but it can speak big things. See how a very small fire can set many trees on fire.

JAMES 3:5

In the end our tongues always
betray symptoms of soul sickness.
KAREN BURTON MAINS

This poor man cried, and the Lord heard him.
And He saved him out of all his troubles.

PSALM 34:6

We must take our troubles to the Lord...but we must do more than that: we must leave them there.
HANNAH WHITALL SMITH

In God I have put my trust. I will not be afraid. What can man do to me?
PSALM 56:11

The kind of trust God wants us to have cannot be learned in comfort and ease.
ANNE GRAHAM LOTZ

Jesus said, "I am the Way and the Truth and the Life. No one can go to the Father except by Me."

JOHN 14:6

The Bible presents true truth, truth that is unchanging, truth that fits in with what exists, truth that answers the questions of life.
EDITH SCHAEFFER

We do not use those things to fight with that the world uses. We use the things God gives to fight with and they have power. Those things God gives to fight with destroy the strong-places of the devil.

2 CORINTHIANS 10:4

No truce while the foe is unconquered;
No laying the armor down!
FANNY CROSBY

I am happy to be weak and have troubles
so I can have Christ's power in me.
2 CORINTHIANS 12:9

God has always allowed man's weakness to validate man's immeasurable need of His redemption and His sufficiency.
MARY SOUTHERLAND

They trust in their riches, and are proud of all they have. No man can save his brother. No man can pay God enough to save him.

PSALM 49:6–7

By finding purpose—bringing it out in our-
selves and in others and putting it to good use,
we find true wealth—a wealth that stock market
downturns or economic slumps cannot take away.
ELLIE KAY

"For I know the plans I have for you," says the Lord, *"plans for well-being and not for trouble, to give you a future and a hope."*

JEREMIAH 29:11

Nothing can happen to a child of God outside the will of God.
JILL BRISCOE

Christ is the power and wisdom of God to those who are chosen to be saved from the punishment of sin for both Jews and Greeks.

1 CORINTHIANS 1:24

Being wise and being knowledgeable are two different things. But when knowledge begins with an understanding of God's character, our wisdom will continue to grow by merely acting on what we know.
VICKI KUYPER

"But you will receive power when the Holy Spirit comes into your life. You will tell about Me in the city of Jerusalem and over all the countries of Judea and Samaria and to the ends of the earth."

ACTS 1:8

I am convinced that believers who are effective in witnessing have most likely been arrested by grace. Not only do they understand it theologically, they have experienced it firsthand.
CHRISTINE WOOD

"God has helped me. To this day I have told these things to the people who are well-known and to those not known."

ACTS 26:22

Are you winning souls for Jesus?
Does your life example prove
Him to be the precious Savior
Sacrificed because of love?
CARRIE BRECK

Who can find a good wife? For she is worth far more than rubies that make one rich.

PROVERBS 31:10

We are happiest when our openhearted friendship with our husband is a strong and sturdy vine that carries the nutrients we both need and desire.
SUE PATTON THOELE

The wise woman builds her house, but the foolish woman tears it down with her own hands.

PROVERBS 14:1

In order to learn what it means to be a woman,
we must start with the One who made her.
ELISABETH ELLIOT

The heavens were made by the Word of the Lord. All the stars were made by the breath of His mouth.

PSALM 33:6

*God hung the universe with words. Everything
you will ever see, touch or taste had its genesis in
a word from God. You exist because God spoke.*
FAWN PARISH

Our words to such people are that they should be quiet and go to work. They should eat their own food.

2 THESSALONIANS 3:12

When the precepts and example of Jesus Christ fully interpermeate society, to labor with the hands will be regarded not only as a duty but a privilege.
CATHERINE BEECHER

Rest in the Lord and be willing to wait for Him. Do not trouble yourself when all goes well with the one who carries out his sinful plans.

PSALM 37:7

Concern draws us to God.
Worry pulls us from him.
JOANNA WEAVER

"For wherever your riches are, your heart will be there also."

MATTHEW 6:21

*Desire and intention are the most
dynamic of our faculties; they do work.
They are the true explorers of the Infinite,
the instruments of our ascents to God.*
EVELYN UNDERHILL

"We are not asking this of You because we are right or good, but because of Your great loving-pity."

DANIEL 9:18